Carcinology

Book of COLORS

A Rainbow of Crustaceans

AO PRESS

Jessica Lee Anderson

Paperback ISBN: 978-1-964078-48-9

To readers of all ages and stages! - JLA

Crustaceans are often multi-colored, so have fun pointing out the variety of colors in addition to the featured colors! Photos are not to scale.

Photo credits, left to right, top to bottom: Front cover: Jenhung Huang (Peacock Mantis Shrimp); Interior cover: Life On White (Rainbow/Patriot Crab); Copyright page: Tim Wijgerde (Hermit Crab); Dedication page: EzumeImages; p. 4: Frankhuang, membio, bdspn; p. 5: Tammy616, Mlenny, Tomasz Dutkiewicz; p. 6:_wilitocricri, Erdal Erdal, cbpix; p. 7: Life On White, Edward Bibbey, hansgertbroeder; p. 8: Rixie, KiaOlsson, NNehring; p. 9: hansgertbroeder, mrbfaust, Сергей Щербина; p. 10: vojce, bdspnimage, jacktheflipper; p. 11: Dibas, lilithlita, marcouliana; p. 12: Andrej Resetniak, Jeffry S.S.; p. 13: IMNATURE, Staras, Prarinya Thonghyad; p. 14: Weber, Eduardo Baena, NNehring; p. 15: Dan Olsen, TS YEW, Mongkolchon Akesin; p. 16: Ian_Redding, Leamus, S.Rohrlach; p. 17: castillodominici, Wan Yong Chong, Gokul Krishnan; p. 18: Sunnypics-oz, micro_photo, Joesboy; p. 19: mauriziobiso, Goldfinch4ever, clumpner; p. 20: Kridsadar Sanyear, Deborah Maxemow, yl413100419; p. 21: Scott O'Neill, drmakete, Arkadij-sh; p. 22: Brett_Hondow, piyomix, kazoka30; p. 23: Sergii_Trofymchuk, scubaluna, Sofroni Maria's Images; p. 24: robertdewit66, NNehring, membio; p. 25: y-studio, choicegraphx, Arnaud Abadie; p. 26: Kridsadar Sanyear, Suriyapong Koktong, hypotekyfidler; p. 27: slowmotiongli, neryxcom, Yupaluk Phangpun; p. 28: Raymond Lau, mantaphoto, Andrej Resetniak; p. 29: phototrip, Luca Gialdini, DaveBluck; 30: Luca Gialdini, John M. Chase, Нина Дроздова; p. 31: naturediver, herbie goller, johnandersonphoto; p. 32: hansgertbroeder, Thierry Eidenweil, Edward Snow; p. 33: Tammy616, fntproject, Amanda Coetzee; p. 34: Michael Anderson; Back cover (Spotted Crab): amysart

This Book Belongs to:

_____

Carcinology is the study of crustaceans like barnacles, crabs, lobsters, pill bugs, and more.

Hermit crab

Red

Crayfish

Japanese spider crabs

Crustaceans have a hard outer shell and a body with segments (arthropod). They have two pair of sensory feelers on their heads called antennae.

Red cherry shrimp

Red

Spiny lobster

Crustaceans range in size from tiny parasites to larger species like lobsters and crabs.

Christmas Island red crab

Splendid red spooner crab

Orange

Painted ghost crab

Hermit crab

Crustaceans have a hard covering on the outside of their bodies called an exoskeleton.

Red hairy hermit crab

Orange

American lobster

Exoskeletons ("outside skeletons") offer crustaceans protection and support.

Orange magnificent isopod

Orangutan crab

Yellow

Japanese spider crab

Golden ghost crab

Many crustaceans have ten legs and three body segments (head, thorax, and abdomen).

Water hoglouse (magnified)

Yellow

Crowned coral crab

A crustacean's legs usually attach to the mid-section (thorax).

Fiddler crab

Yellow cherry shrimp

Green

Green emerald crab

Green jade shrimp

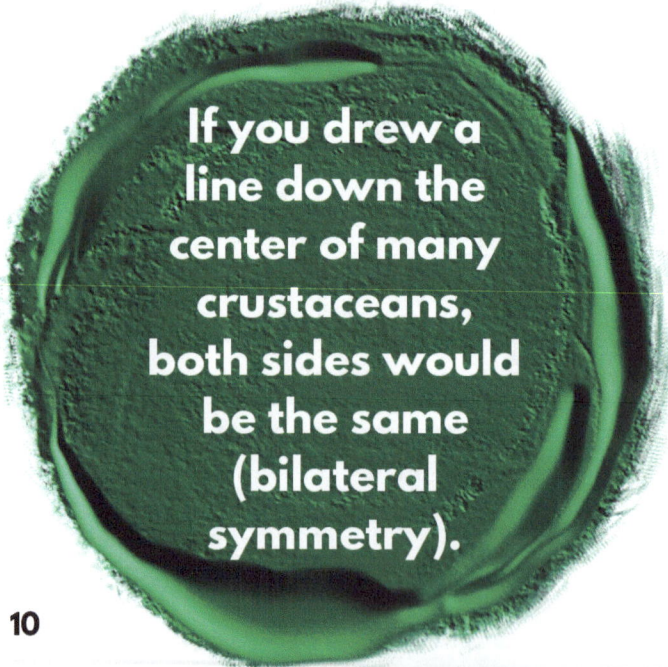

If you drew a line down the center of many crustaceans, both sides would be the same (bilateral symmetry).

Green crab

Green

Crayfish

Crustaceans have jointed appendages (flexible sections) that allow them to move.

Reef hermit crab

Sand hopper

Blue

There are over 50,000 crustacean species found all over the world!

Aura blue tiger shrimp

Blue bolt shrimp

Everglades crayfish

Blue

Blue lobster

Blue dream shrimp

Blue flower crab

Crustaceans live in a variety of environments from deserts to icy landscapes in Antarctica.

Purple

Fiddler crab

Dungeness crab

The majority of crustaceans are marine, meaning they live in and around the ocean.

Purple shore crab

Purple

Purple vampire crab

Some species like crayfish live in freshwater while others like woodlice live on land (terrestrial).

Purple crab

Meder's mangrove crab

Pink

Rosy woodlouse

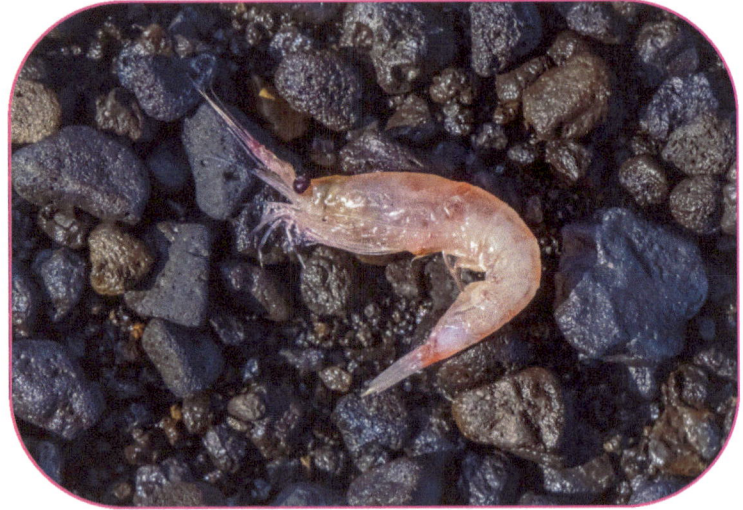
Antarctic krill

Crustaceans like copepods, krill, and brine shrimp are a type of plankton, an important food source for many animals.

Brine shrimp (magnified)

Pink

Pink ghost crab

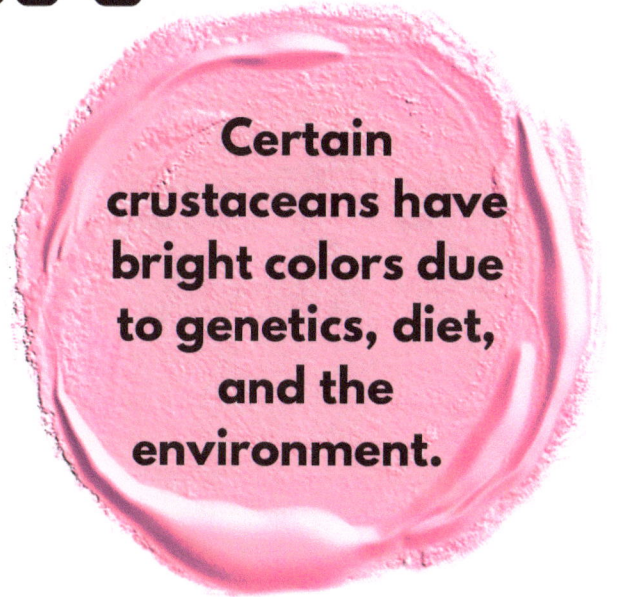

Certain crustaceans have bright colors due to genetics, diet, and the environment.

Candy crab

Cherry shrimp

17

Black

Giant mud crab

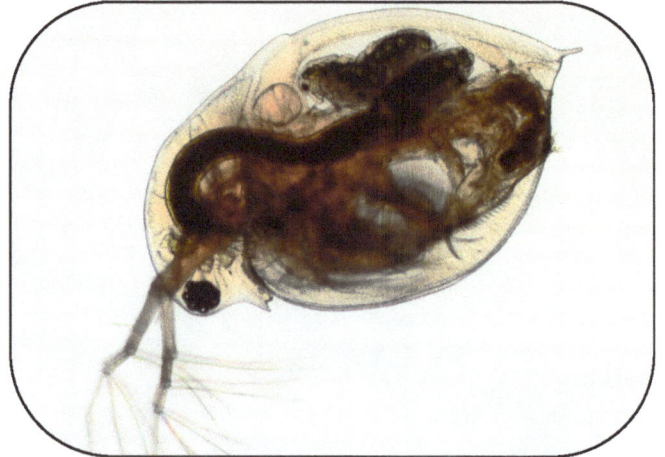
Water flea (magnified)

Some crustaceans eat both plants and animals (omnivores) while others eat only algae (herbivores).

Ghost crab

Black

Caridina shrimp

Species like woodlice, shrimps, crabs, and lobsters are important decomposers, meaning they break down dead matter.

Woodlice (pill bugs)

Coconut crab

White

Magic potion isopods

Gooseneck barnacles

Barnacles are marine crustaceans that might look like snails, but they have more in common with crabs.

White mantis shrimp

White

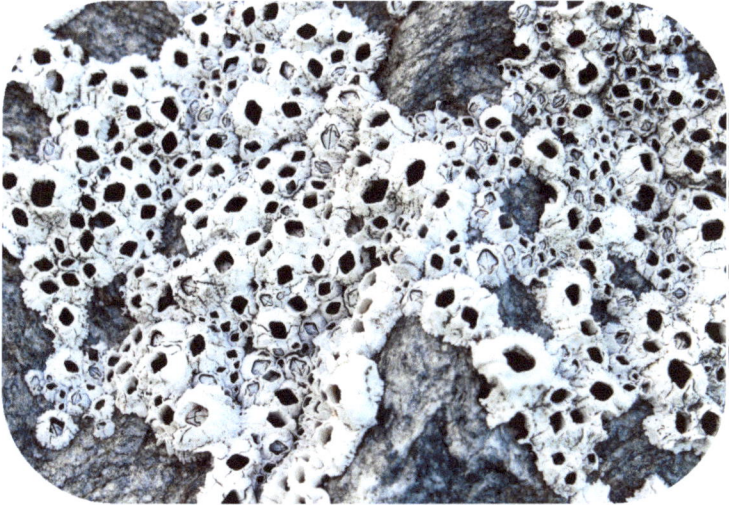

Rock barnacles

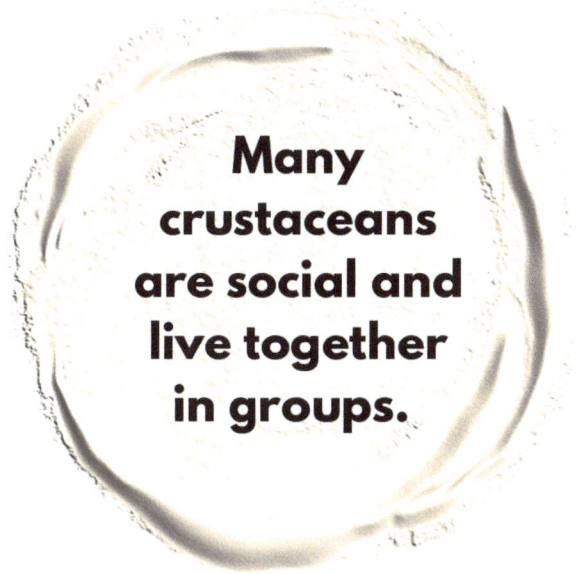

Many crustaceans are social and live together in groups.

Ghost crab

Red Sea land hermit crab

Gray

Woodlouse (pill bug)

Titan acorn barnacles

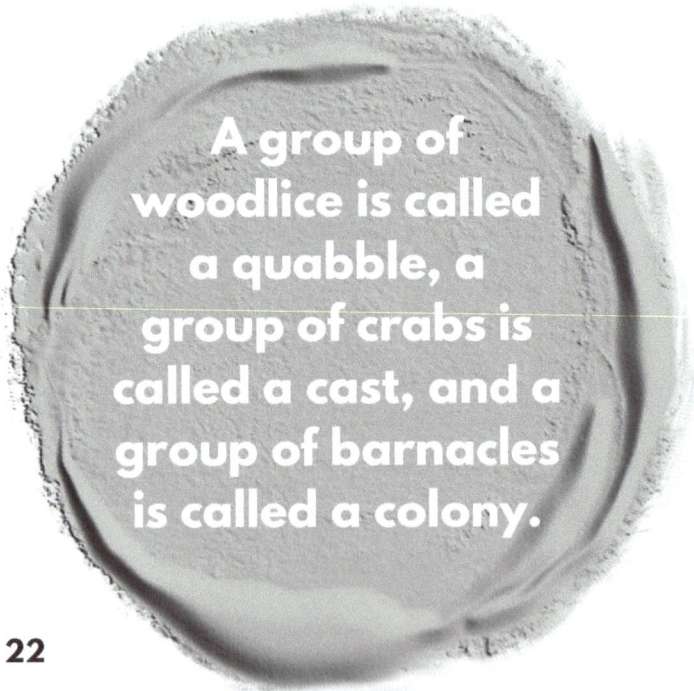

A group of woodlice is called a quabble, a group of crabs is called a cast, and a group of barnacles is called a colony.

Giant mud crab

Gray

Copepod (magnified)

Scientists are continuing to make discoveries about crustaceans, like recently discovering a new species in a deep-sea trench.

Carinate snapping shrimp

Giant isopod

Brown

Spiny lobster

Copepod (magnified)

Crustaceans are an important source of food for people as well as other animals.

Poli's stellate barnacles

Brown

Snow crab

Crustaceans help recycle nutrients in the ecosystem and bring balance as both predators and prey.

Calico crab

Louisana crayfish

COLOR Combinations

Lemon blue isopods

Can you describe the colors and patterns of these isopods?

Rubber ducky isopod

Woodlouse

COLOR Combinations

Violet-spotted reef lobster

Australian redclaw crayfish

Ghost crayfish

How are the colors of the crustaceans similar and different?

COLOR Combinations

What are some colors and features you notice about these different shrimp species?

Crystal red shrimp

Peacock mantis shrimp

Shadow panda shrimp

COLOR Combinations

Fairy shrimp

Stimpson's snapping shrimp

Harlequin shrimp

What are some things you notice about the shapes, colors, and patterns?

29

COLOR Combinations

How are these colors and features similar or different?

Sally lightfoot crab

Maryland blue crab

Rainbow crab

COLOR Combinations

Puget Sound king crab

Porcelain crab

Yellowline arrow crab

What do you notice about the shapes, colors, and features of the crabs?

COLOR Combinations

Can you describe the colors and patterns of these crabs?

Boxer crab

Zebra crab

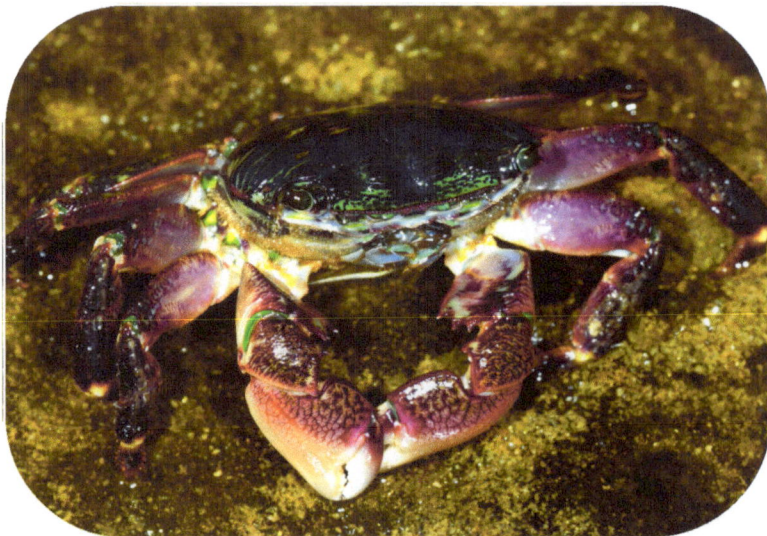

Striped shore crab

COLOR Combinations

Hairy hermit crab

Red land crab

Clown crab

Why do you think the colors, shapes, and features of a crustacean matters?

Jessica Lee Anderson is an award-winning author of over 100 books for young readers including the NAOMI NASH chapter book series. Jessica loves spending time in nature and exploring the outdoors with her husband, Michael, and their daughter, Ava! Jessica loves going admiring crustaceans (especially when snorkeling). You can learn more about Jessica by visiting **www.jessicaleeanderson.com**.

Check out these other books:

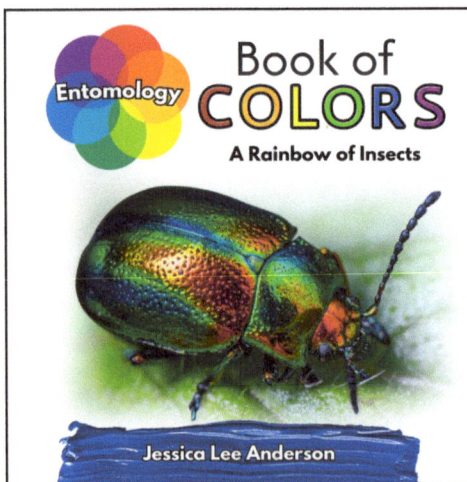

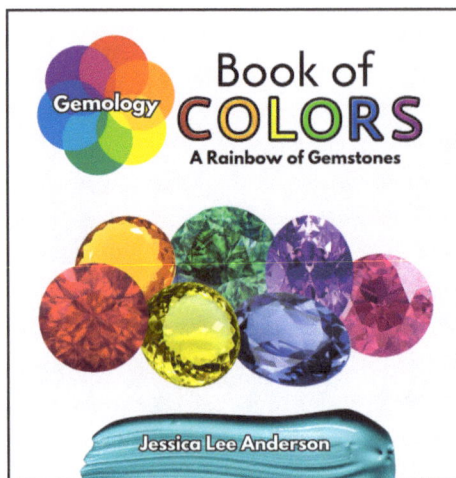

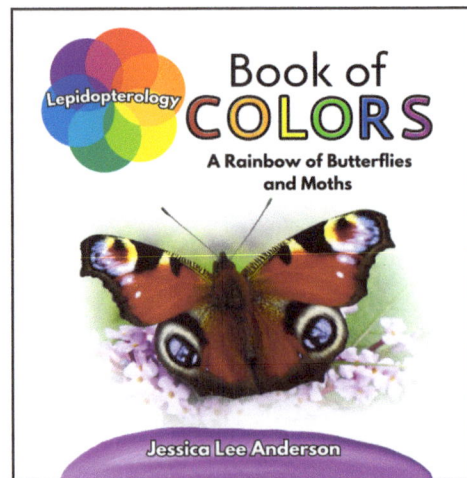

Entomology
Book of COLORS
A Rainbow of Insects
Jessica Lee Anderson

Gemology
Book of COLORS
A Rainbow of Gemstones
Jessica Lee Anderson

Lepidopterology
Book of COLORS
A Rainbow of Butterflies and Moths
Jessica Lee Anderson